YO-BPW-431

Copyright © by Harcourt, Inc.

Printed in the United States of America

ISBN-13: 978-0-15-352852-1
ISBN-10: 0-15-352852-4

1 2 3 4 5 6 7 8 9 10   179   11 10 09 08 07 06

Harcourt
SCHOOL PUBLISHERS

Visit *The Learning Site!* www.harcourtschool.com

Small Find, Big Change

Can you imagine finding a piece of gold in your backyard? That's just what happened to a man named John Sutter in 1848. Sutter had come to the United States from Switzerland. He went west to California to build a large ranch.

In the early 1800s, there were not many settlers in the western part of the United States. There was plenty of land to build on. In California, John Sutter owned a large ranch and fort. He bought cows and hired a lot of people to work for him.

One person he hired was a man named James Marshall. Marshall was in charge of building a sawmill just north of Sutter's fort. The sawmill would provide the wood Sutter needed.

Sutter's Fort

John Sutter

2

Workers at Sutter's Mill found a gold nugget.

On January 24, 1848, Marshall and some workers were building the sawmill. Looking down into the river, a worker noticed something shiny. He bent down to take a closer look.

The worker picked up a small rock from the river bottom. Up close, it looked like a piece of gold! As he looked in the shallow waters of the river, he saw other pea-sized pieces of gold scattered all around.

Marshall took some of the pieces back to John Sutter. First, Sutter and Marshall tested the metal to make sure it was really gold. Then, they decided to keep the gold a secret from other people. They did not want too many people to come west in search of gold.

Gold Fever!

Sutter's secret did not last. Soon, news of the gold discovery at Sutter's Mill had spread. At first, many people did not believe the stories they heard. But then, a merchant in San Francisco named Sam Brannan stepped in.

Samuel Brannan

Brannan had a clever plan. First, he bought every gold-digging tool he could find. Then, he ran through the streets, showing people a bottle of gold dust. He told them it was gold found at John Sutter's mill. Soon everyone wanted to go looking for gold, and they needed tools.

Brannan had plenty of tools to sell, and the prices kept going up. Metal pans that cost 20 cents on Monday might cost $5 by Tuesday. Brannan made $36,000 in less than three months!

An advertisement for mining tools

Miner's Gold Pan.

44500 Miners' Gold Pans. Polished iron. 15¼x-2½; weight, 2 pounds.

Each...........................$0.30

4

Sam Brannan started what would become the California gold rush. Almost overnight, "gold fever," the desire to hunt for gold, hit people all over the country.

Farmers and city dwellers wanted to come to California to get rich quick. All across the country, people left their fields and closed up their shops.

Because so many people headed west in 1849, these gold seekers are called "forty-niners." About 80,000 forty-niners flooded into California in the first year.

Some forty-niners were rich. Some were poor. They had worked at many different jobs before leaving for California. At first, most gold miners were Americans, but later they came from all over the world. Many came from China.

This illustration shows gold miners working in California.

The Journey West

How did all of these people get to California? The forty-niners could travel by land or by sea. Many people from the east coast decided to go by sea. They had to sail all the way around the southern tip of South America and then north to California. The trip took at least six months. It was not an easy one. Most people became seasick. Food on the ships was often full of bugs.

Some people tried a shortcut. They sailed to Central America and then crossed Central America on land. On the other side, they waited for a ship to pick them up. The wait could take weeks or even months. Many travelers became sick. Some did not reach California at all.

THE WAY OUT WEST

Some inventors tried to come up with other ways to get to the west coast. One idea was an airplane lifted by huge balloons, but this invention never left the ground. Another idea was a "wind wagon," a cross between a wagon and a sailboat. But wind power wasn't reliable, and steering was a problem. The wind wagon was never used.

Overland to California

Legend:
→ California Trail → Santa Fe Trail
→ Old Spanish Trail ■ Fort
→ Oregon Trail — Present-day border

Land routes to California

People who started from the middle of the country traveled mostly over land to reach California. Even though this trip was shorter, it could take just as long as going by sea. It was dangerous, too.

The overland route was called the Oregon-California Trail. Moving along in covered wagons, the travelers only went about 2 miles per hour. Sometimes, so many wagons traveled on the Oregon-California Trail that it was like a huge traffic jam!

Conditions along the trail were very bad. Along many parts of the trail, there was little water. By the time the forty-niners got within a few hundred miles of California, many of them had practically nothing to drink.

Hard Times for the Forty-Niners

Most of the gold in the world is buried in hard rock, deep underground. But the gold in California was closer to Earth's surface. It was easier to get at. All a person needed was time, hard work, luck, and a few simple tools.

Besides that, the gold in California was free for the taking. California had just become a state, so there was no state government yet. No rules existed about who could or could not take the gold.

For these reasons, people thought that digging for gold in California would be a fast way to get rich. But getting rich turned out not to be so easy. This was especially true for people who did not get to California right away.

Miners worked hard in difficult conditions.

8

A mining camp in California

A gold miner's life was hard. Most miners were far from home. They had left their families behind, promising to return soon with gold.

A year after the first pieces of gold were found, most miners were frustrated. Food was almost as hard to find as gold in the mining camps. Some forty-niners slept under blankets hanging over poles. Others lived in caves in the ground or in tiny shacks.

Few women lived in mining camps. One who did was Louise Clapp. Along with her doctor husband, Clapp lived in mining camps in northern California from 1851 to 1852. In letters written to her sister, Clapp described life in the camps. Her letters were published in a magazine under the name "Dame Shirley."

Supply and Demand

Because there were so many consumers and so few supplies in the mining camps, everything cost a lot of money. Many merchants took advantage of this situation.

Merchants sold supplies and food to the miners at very high prices. A single egg might cost 50 cents. Along the Oregon-California Trail, forty-niners might pay as much as $100 for a glass of water!

The low supply and the high demand during the gold rush made many merchants wealthy. In fact, merchants were more likely to get rich than the miners themselves. The miners might not be able to find gold, but the merchants could always sell their products.

This cartoon illustrates how expensive goods had become in California.

Women could also make a lot of money in the mining camps by selling household services. Most of the men had left their wives far behind. There were not very many women in the camps. The few women who were there charged high prices for cooking and cleaning.

Thomas Houseworth's store provided services to miners in San Francisco in the 1860s.

It was the first time that many women in the United States were able to make their own money. They might make five or ten dollars for cooking a meal, or eight dollars for washing a bundle of clothes. Women could run boarding houses and make $200 a week.

Many former African American slaves also found new opportunities in California. Mifflin Gibbs opened a shoe store in San Francisco during the gold rush. He used some of the money he earned to help buy the freedom of enslaved African Americans.

Mifflin Gibbs

The End of Gold Fever

A miner could spend ten hours a day in the icy water, digging and sifting through rocks, looking for glimmers of gold. It was very hard work, and most of the miners were not finding much.

By the middle of 1849, most of the easy-to-reach gold was gone. There was still gold in California, but it was buried deep in the ground. The miners had to dig deeper to find it. They needed more-advanced tools to help them reach the gold.

Some miners gave up and headed back home. Their dreams of striking it rich were over. Other miners stayed in California. Many became farmers and made new lives for themselves.

Miners used water from powerful hoses to reach gold deeper in the ground. This was called hydraulic mining.

A California river clogged with debris from hydraulic mining.

And what happened to John Sutter? Did he get rich from the gold found on his land?

The answer is no. The gold seekers who rushed to California trampled his land. They killed many of his cattle. They stole his goods. He left California and never made any money from the gold that was found on his land.

The gold rush also caused problems for Californians of Mexican heritage, called Californios. Some Californios did get rich in the early days of the gold rush. Over time, however, the crowds of miners ruined their land.

Native Americans also did not benefit from the gold rush. Miners eager to find gold often invaded Native American lands. This led to conflicts between Native Americans and miners.

Another Gold Rush!

California was not the only place to have a gold rush in the 1800s. Gold was found far north of California, too, in the territory called Alaska.

Alaska was not yet part of the United States. People had to travel through Canada to get there. There were many gold discoveries in Alaska. The first discovery was in Juneau in 1880.

Chief Kowee

Chief Kowee, a native Alaskan from a group called the Auk, was one of the first people to find gold in Juneau. Chief Kowee wanted to help his people profit from the gold there.

Miners in the Klondike had to deal with cold, snowy weather.

However, Chief Kowee and his tribe did not become wealthy from his discovery. They were only given 100 blankets for finding the first gold.

The largest Alaskan gold rush was in 1896. In that year, gold was discovered in an area called the Klondike. Advertisements in magazines and newspapers spread the news about all the gold that was available in this area.

Traveling to the Klondike was even more dangerous than going to California. And once they got there, gold seekers faced avalanches, diseases, and crime. But many people were willing to face the dangers in the hope of getting rich quickly. Between 1897 and 1898, more than 60,000 people rushed to the Klondike, looking for gold. A lot of people caught "gold fever," but in the end, very few got rich.

The front cover of the *Klondike News* shows how much gold the miners found in 1898.

Think and Respond

1. How was gold first discovered in California?

2. How did people get to California to look for gold?

3. What was life like for the gold miners?

4. Why did the merchants often make more money than the gold miners?

5. Why do you think "gold fever" hit so many people?

 # Activity

Imagine that you are living in a California mining camp. You could be a miner, a merchant, or a businesswoman. Write a letter to your family back east. Tell them about your life in the camp.